C000018110

WAIT AND TRUST

Other titles by Angela Ashwin
published by Eagle

Patterns Not Padlocks
Patterns in Prayer (tape)
Wait and See

Copyright © 1997 Angela Ashwin

British Library Cataloguing-in-Publication Data. A
catalogue record for this book is available from the
British Library.

Published by Eagle, an imprint of Inter Publishing
Service (IPS) Ltd, St Nicholas House, 14 The Mount,
Guildford, Surrey GU2 5HN.

Printed in Italy by LEGO
ISBN: 0 86347 208 1

WAIT AND TRUST

Words and pictures leading into stillness with God

ANGELA ASHWIN

eagle

Guildford, Surrey

This book is dedicated to
Sister Pamela Hayes RSCJ

CONTENTS

PREFACE

This project has resulted in all sorts of unexpected bonuses for me, especially in working with the artists, several of whom I would not otherwise have come to know. I am most grateful to Sophie Hacker, Margaret Neve, Paul Judson, Sr Anna SSM, Sr Ann Wilson OSB, Mother Rosemary SLG, Sr Margaret Tournour RSCJ, Sr Rachel Clare OHP, Pauline K Green, Graeme Bland and Kay Gibbons, who also did the beautiful calligraphy. They have all been marvellously sensitive to the nature of this book, and very patient when I wanted to work through themes with them and suggest modifications of the pictures.

Many others have helped, including Anne and Peter Lepine, who prayed with some of the texts as they evolved and came back with wise and perceptive comments. I am also grateful to my editor, David Wavre at Eagle, for his support and encouragement throughout the long gestation period of these meditations.

INTRODUCTION

'When I sit down to pray at home my brain
refuses to quieten down.'

'Most of my life is spent trying to squeeze too
much work into too little time, so I find the long
gaps during a silent retreat quite unnerving.'

'My prayer-life has got into a rut and I need
more silence, but I don't know where to start.'

'On a retreat or quiet day there isn't time
to read a whole book, but I still want
something to chew over.'

It was on hearing comments like these that I first
realised the need for some material which was not
too long and could lead people into stillness,
either in private prayer or during quiet days and
retreats. These meditations, and those in the com-
panion volume *Wait and See*, are the result.

I have woven into this collection many of the
themes and images which I myself find helpful
when trying to become inwardly quiet with God.
With each meditation there is a picture, and these
come from several different artists. The resulting
mixture of styles could be a drawback if the books
were intended to be read straight through, from
cover to cover; but each double-page spread is a
unit in its own right, so I hope that the variety will
be an advantage, especially since we all have different tastes and changing moods. (Names of
artists and comments about the text can be found
in the Notes and Acknowledgements at the back of
the book.)

Sometimes you may want to concentrate on the words rather than on the picture – and sometimes the opposite will be true. The important thing is to do whatever comes most naturally.

Common problems

It is reassuring to know that most of us find it difficult to find inner silence when we pray.

Without something to anchor us in stillness, our minds tend to buzz with random memories and thoughts, so that we despair of ever getting rid of our mental chatter.

Or else a period of silence is so tedious that we are tempted to think it all a waste of time. We long for the allotted period to end, but then feel guilty for having even thought that!

8

Or we take so long wondering where to start, which Bible passage to read or what theme to take, that we spend much of our prayer-time fretting, convinced that something else would have been better.

If you have been in any of these situations, I hope that this book will help. There is no set scheme to work through in order to 'achieve' anything, but just a selection of pathways into the unknown world of quiet prayer, where God offers us the gift of himself. Different people will use the meditations in different ways; some will take them as springboards into long periods of silence, while others will want to stay with an idea and simply absorb it at a deep level.

Where?

Find a quiet place. A comfortable upright chair is generally better than a very soft armchair. Or you may prefer to kneel with a prayer-stool, or sit on the floor.

How much time?

It depends what you've got! You may only have five or ten minutes; or you could spend half an hour on a single paragraph. The main thing is TAKE IT SLOWLY. There is nothing to be gained from 'getting through' the text just for the sake of it. Hurrying makes prayer less helpful, not more so. It doesn't matter what point you have reached when you stop.

One line or paragraph at a time

Let the words sink in, from your head to your heart. Linger with each paragraph for as long as you want before moving on. You might find it helpful to use a postcard to cover up the line below the one you are reading, so that your eyes cannot jump ahead.

Repeating a word or phrase

If a certain phrase or thought is especially significant for you, you could stay with it, repeating it quietly to yourself with the rhythm of your breathing. Let the words become part of you, as a source of strength on which to draw during the rest of the day.

Don't be discouraged

Wandering thoughts do not matter as long as your basic intention is to be with God. You cannot measure the value of prayer according to the number of seconds you manage to concentrate, any more than love can be measured in a bottle. Distractions are, after all, things that have emerged from your own heart and mind, so the best thing is simply to give them to God without agitation or guilt. Then you may want to return to a key phrase (see paragraph above) or to use A Pathway into Stillness (page 14) to lead you back into the silence.

Sometimes prayer feels a complete blank. This is all right, and is in no way a sign of 'spiritual failure'. We never know fully what God is doing in us, and his touch and presence are often beyond our comprehension. What counts is our desire to pray and our willingness to be open to him. It is God who has taken the initiative. He has called us and we are simply responding. He is in our darkness and 'unknowing' as much as in the moments of illumination and certainty.

Other ways of praying

While this book is primarily concerned with contemplative prayer, it must be stressed that this is by no means the only way to come close to God. We meet him in busyness as well as in stillness, in liturgical and spontaneous prayer as well as in silence. We all have to find the way or ways of praying which are right for us, and talking with a spiritual director or 'soul-mate' can help in this process of discernment.

Groups

Themes in this book can also be used in prayer groups. For example, one person could read aloud, slowly, the Pathway into Silence on page 14, followed by one of the meditations. The book is then placed at a central point for a time of corporate silence. (If you have a large number of people it helps to have two or three copies available, so that everyone can see the picture easily. Or you could just use the words.) The session can be closed with a simple prayer.

Is contemplative prayer an escape?

People sometimes ask us to justify the time we spend in contemplative prayer. Doing nothing with God can appear suspect in a world where values tend to be measured by productivity and instant results. Yet to be exposed to God is to be in touch with the creative power at the heart of everything. Far from being a cosy escape, deep prayer leads us to give more and more of ourselves to God, and to become increasingly attentive to the pain and needs of the world.

Prayer affects all of life

Times which we set aside just for being with God express something which is true all the time, i.e. that we are always in his presence. People often say that the peace of a prayer-time spills over into the rest of life, and that things are somehow changed. They may grow in self-knowledge, or find they can muster a bit more courage than usual; or perhaps they experience a new sense of the wonder of the natural world. Maria Boulding sums this up well when she says that silence with God '... *seems to grow vaster and more mysterious than ever. But it is light and life for the spirit and it has a curious way of lighting up everything else.*' [1]

Wait and Trust

Prayer is often a matter of waiting. We are not aware of what is happening or where God is leading us, and sometimes we seem to be in complete darkness. This requires trust. The value of our praying does not lie in any good feeling (though that may come as an unexpected gift). What matters is that we persevere, offering to God our loving attention as faithfully as we can. And all prayer draws us closer to Christ, who trusted his Father totally, even through the suffering of the cross.

A final thought

Words can get in the way. But sometimes we need them to lead us into the mystery of God, who is beyond all words and concepts. The meditations in this book will be doing their job, if, like stained-glass windows, they point beyond themselves and allow the divine radiance to pour through, into our hearts.

Postscript

If you have tinnitus (as I do) take heart! Silence is a quality of being, and does not depend on the state of your ears, any more than true vision depends on the state of your eyes. There is a stillness even deeper than the internal noise. We have to stay there in trust, even when we cannot hear pure silence ourselves. God is there.

Book 1: **Wait and Trust** incorporates some of the themes of Lent, Easter and Pentecost.
Book 2: **Wait and See** takes up some themes in the season from Advent to Epiphany.

A Pathway into Stillness
can be used as a springboard
into silence in its own right,
or as a preparation
for one of the meditations
that follow.

Page 15 may be photocopied, so that you can place the words next to a meditation for easy reference, e.g. when your mind has wandered and you want to become inwardly quiet again. This permission applies only to page 15.

A PATHWAY INTO STILLNESS

I recommit myself to this present moment
with God.

I allow my body to become still,

releasing all its tension.

I listen to the sounds around me,

and become aware of the stillness that

encompasses everything.

In the silence

I open my heart to God.

1. ROOTED IN GOD

Blessed are those who trust in the Lord. They are like trees planted by water, sending out their roots by the stream.

Jeremiah 17: 7 - 8

Everything we do and say,
and all our outward behaviour,
springs from our hidden, inner life.

Sometimes we give so much attention
to our external activities, the *fruits* in our lives,
that we neglect the vital *roots* of prayer
upon which everything else depends.

We need to be rooted and grounded in God,
both through our spoken prayers
and in the wordless communion of love.

*Lord, make me like a tree planted by a stream,
drawing on the living water of your presence
in deep-flowing stillness.*

2. WANTING GOD

If you seek the Lord with all your heart, you will truly find him .

Deuteronomy 4:29

Lord, beneath all the concerns on the surface of my mind, I long to be in close communion with you.

Even when my desire for you is swamped by many preoccupations, I still know in my heart that I need you more than anything else.

You are my beloved friend,
and nothing can take that away from you.
I was the one who planted in you this longing
for me,
like a seed in the earth.
The very fact you are turning to me now
shows that your desire for me has been growing,
even if you did not realise it.

Your very desire
is itself prayer.

Remember that I made you in my image –
so your yearning for me
reflects my great longing for you.

*In silence I reach out to God,
in this mystery of mutual desire.*

18

3. WAITING

For God alone my soul waits in silence;
from him comes my salvation.

Psalm 62:1

My seeking him would have been in vain if,
beyond all time, he had not sought me.

Carlo Carretto

I wait
and I trust,
hiding nothing from you, my God,
holding back nothing from you.

I wait
not for a message
or a special experience,
or even a meaning.

I simply wait
in your presence,
because the waiting is everything;

and when I wait for you
I am found by you.

4. SIMPLY BEING

Contemplative prayer is a matter of being:
being in stillness,
being in God;
not achieving anything
or trying to find words,
but simply being.

O God,
you are Yahweh, 'I am who I am,'
the One who Is.
My very existence is your gift to me.
I am here
before you
now.

Be

Still ,

and

know

that I am

GOD.

Psalm 46 : 10

5. LOVING, NOT GRASPING

Even in the deepest human relationships there is an element of mystery. When we love someone, there are always things about the other person that we do not know and can never possess.

It is all the more so with God, who is infinitely beyond anything we could imagine. If we were able to grasp him, he would not be God.

Thus prayer is often a kind of waiting, remaining silent in God's awesome presence. It is a state of not-having, not-knowing.

And as we wait in loving expectation, God draws us to himself, whether we are aware of it or not.

Lord.I have loved you with an everlasting love, says the

Jeremiah 31:3

6. CARVED OUT

I am poured out like water,
and all my bones
are out of
joint;

my heart within my breast
is like melting wax.

Psalm 22:14

When you pray during a time of trouble or conflict, you will probably be more aware of your pain than of anything else. Easy words and pious platitudes won't do. You need both the freedom to express how you feel, and the strength to face the pain so that it does not become a destructive energy inside you.

It is as if you have been carved out, like a bamboo shoot which has been made into a tube so that water can flow through it. You could ask God to be the one who hollows you out, removes your bitterness and flows through your pain himself, as healing and life-giving water.

Carve me out, Lord,
and flow through my wounds yourself.

Save me from bitterness and
make me into a channel of your love for others.

7. PENITENCE

Christ,
your offering of yourself
was total.
You could not have loved us more.

My offering is fragmented, flawed, incomplete.

I place mine in yours.

He
was
wounded
for our transgressions,
bruised for our sins ;
upon him was the chastisement that
made us whole,
and with
his
stripes
we
are
healed.

Isaiah 53:5

29

8. HEALING

God did not spare his own Son, but gave him up
for us all. In this we are more than conquerors
through him who loved us.
I am sure that neither death, nor life,
nor powers, nor height, nor depth, nor
anything else in all creation, can
separate us from the love of God in Jesus Christ.

Romans 8:32, 37-9

Jesus,
from your cross
light, healing and hope
pour out onto us all.

I hold before you
those who are living with
heartbreak
anxiety
guilt
illness
injustice
or despair.

I remain before you
in silence
for all who need your love.

9. AFTER GREAT PAIN

Joseph of Arimathea took down the body of Jesus,
wrapped it in a linen cloth, and laid it in a rock-hewn
tomb. The women who had come with him from
Galilee saw how his body was laid. And on the
sabbath day they rested.

Luke 23:53-6

Stunned, numb,
yet strangely quiet.

It is finished.
It is over.

On the cross
Love came face to face with evil
and was not overcome.
Darkness tried its worst
but is now in retreat.

Jesus,
I open up my pain to you.
You have already borne it with me.
You will not leave me bereft.

In this moment of calm
I trust you and I wait ...

10. RESURRECTION

*I saw one like a Son of Man ; his eyes were like a flame
of fire, and his face was like the sun shining in full strength.*

Revelation 1 : 13, 14, 16

Risen Christ,
I adore you.
Your presence
is an explosion of light
breaking out
into every corner of our pain-racked world.

You have plunged into our darkness,
transforming our hate, evil and sin
into an energy of divine love.

You break the bounds of reason.
You shatter our neat formulas.
You fill and overflow our doctrines.

You are
Christ,
dazzling,
radiant,
unfettered and all-loving,
fire we cannot grasp,
yet most intimate mystery.

11. PEACE

Calm my restless brain,
loosen the knots of tension
and touch my heart,
so that your peace may permeate
my whole being
as gently as flowing water.

PEACE
I
leave
with
you,

my
PEACE
I give to you;

not as the world gives
do
I give to you.

John 14:27

12. THE FIRE OF LOVE

When the day of Pentecost had come, they were altogether in one place. And suddenly there came the sound of a great wind, and tongues, as of fire, rested on each of them, and they were filled with the Holy Spirit.

Acts 2:1-3

Holy Spirit,
fire of love,
consume all that is rotten in me,
and change me from the inside.

Holy Spirit,
Comforter,
melt all that is cold and hard in me,
and soothe my hurts in your warmth.

Holy Spirit,
transforming power,
light up my heart
and take possession of me,
so that I may become flame.

Fire is kindled when God's self-emptying in Christ
meets our self-emptying in prayer.
St. Isaac the Syrian (seventh century)

13. WATER OF LIFE

O God, you are my God, eagerly do I seek you;
my soul thirsts for you, my flesh faints for you,
in a dry and weary land where there is no water.

Psalm 63:1-2

In this moment of quiet
I pause,
so that I can stop giving out
and have a chance to receive.

I move from complexity to simplicity,
from busyness to stillness.

I long for you, Lord.
I thank you
that you freely pour your Spirit into my heart,
not because of anything I have done
but because, quite simply, I am here,
with all my weaknesses and failures.

Cleanse me,
renew me,
and refresh me in your unimaginable love.

14. THE SHEPHERD

THE
LORD
IS MY SHEPHERD,
I
SHALL WANT
FOR
NOTHING.

PSALM 23:1

Shepherd of my soul,
find me again.

Anoint me
and show me the way.

Stay with me when it is dark.

Bring me to the quiet place beside still waters
where I may rest,
trusting in the ancient promise of
your steadfast love.

15. THE FISH

It has been said
that when we try to find God by anxious searching
we are like fish swimming round and round,
furiously hunting for the ocean.

All that is needed
is that we surrender into the gentle
flow and movement
of God's presence all around us,
and swim freely.

IN YOU, LORD,
I LIVE

AND MOVE

AND HAVE
MY BEING .

FROM ACTS 17:28

16. REFLECTION

And
there
was
Silence
in
heaven.

Revelation 8:1

There is a stillness in God.

Because we are made in his image
we can echo his silence
as well as reflect his love.

Nothing in all creation is so like God
as stillness.
In limpid souls God beholds his own image;
he rests in them, and they in him.
Meister Eckhart (1260–1327)

17. REST

Come to me all who labour and are heavy laden,
and I will give you rest.

Matthew 11:28

Lord, when I am weary
and have nothing left of my own to offer,
help me to find rest in you.

I will take the weight off your shoulders.
Let your spirit fly free for a while,
resting on the breath of my Spirit.

You do not have to say or do anything -
simply abandon yourself to me.

I am with you
always.

I am beneath you and around you,
and I understand.

I will never forsake you.
In your old age I shall still be the same;
when your hair is grey I shall still carry you.

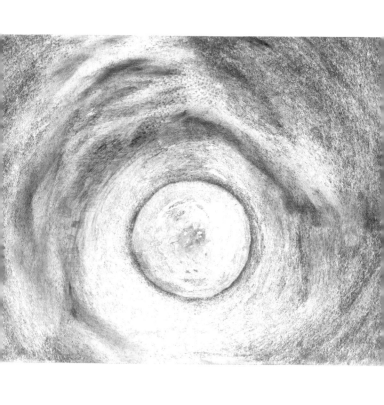

18. THE CENTRE

In returning and in rest you shall be saved;
in quietness and trust shall be your strength.

Isaiah 30:15

Go deep
into the core of your being,
allowing surface things to fall away.

Return to the centre,
to the inner room of your soul,
and there let your spirit meet
the infinite love of God.

Wherever you are
and whatever circumstances you are in,
you can always return
to this hidden place of quietness and rest
at the heart of your heart.

19. WRITE ON MY HEART

THE LORD SAYS, I WILL PUT MY LAW WITHIN THEM
AND I WILL WRITE IT ON THEIR HEARTS.

JEREMIAH 31:33

In the fourteenth century, the teacher
Meister Eckhart
said that, when we pray,
we should make our hearts empty and ready for
God to write on,
like a newly-cleaned wax tablet.

Blessedness, he explained, lies not in
our own actions,
but in our capacity to allow God to act in us.

My God,
I am yours.
Do whatever you want in me.
Inscribe your love in my soul.

20. NOTHING AND EVERYTHING

Blessed are the poor in spirit ; for theirs is the kingdom of heaven.

Matthew 5:3

Being alone with God
means that I can hide nothing.
Any facades I might put on for the benefit of
others
disappear.
Distractions into which I could deliberately
escape
have to go.

I stand here, naked and unprotected before God,
aware only of my poverty.

And God comes to me
at the point where I most need him,
pouring his warmth into my hurts and fears,
and his love into those parts of myself which I
cannot even name.

And that is everything.

21. THE SEED

UNLESS A GRAIN OF WHEAT FALLS INTO THE EARTH
AND DIES, IT REMAINS JUST A SINGLE GRAIN; BUT
IF IT DIES, IT BEARS MUCH FRUIT.

JOHN 12:24

Sometimes God asks us to let go of our
own concerns,
leave self behind,
and follow his call into the depths of prayer.

Then we become like a seed falling into the
ground,
plunging into God's fathomless love.

It is not for us to worry about the fruits of our
praying.
All that is needed
is that we are there,
in God.

Lord, I abandon myself to you.
Dissolve all that is stiff and hard in my heart,
so that the 'self' in me
may be lost, found and made new
in the good earth of deep silence.

57

22. EARLY MORNING –
A FRESH BEGINNING

O GOD YOU ARE MY GOD ; EARLY WILL I SEEK YOU .

PSALM 63:1

If you go out early on a clear, bright morning, there can be a sense of peaceful expectation in the air, as if all living things are saying,
    'Here is the gift of a new day,
        fresh,
        unspoilt,
        full of potential,
        vulnerable in your hands
        yet freely entrusted to you.
    Can you see the glory and hear the stillness?'

Lord, I praise you
for the miracle of life itself.
May I never take for granted
the fragile splendour of your world.

Help me to listen
to the songs and silences of creation.

With you every moment is a new beginning.
Come into my soul
like the quiet sunrise.

I wait
and I trust ...

NOTES, ACKNOWLEDGEMENTS AND PICTURE CREDITS

Introduction
Maria Boulding, *The Coming of God* (London, SPCK, 1994) p179.

1. Rooted in God
Ref. 'May Christ dwell in your hearts through faith; that you, being rooted and grounded in love, may know the breadth and length and depth of the love of Christ, and be filled with all the fullness of God' (Ephesians 3:17–18). Artist: © Paul Judson.

2. Wanting God
Artist: © Pauline K Green.

3. Waiting
The quote by Carlo Carretto is from *Letters from the Desert* (London, DLT, 1972) p 37. Artist: © Sophie Hacker.

4. Simply Being
The Hebrew root of the name 'Yahweh' is the verb 'to be'. In Exodus 3:14–15 God says to Moses, 'I AM WHO I AM. Thus you shall say to the Israelites, "I AM" has sent you.' The seven great 'I am' sayings of Jesus in the Fourth Gospel develop this. Artist: © Sister Margaret Tournour RSCJ.

5. Loving, not Grasping
Artist: © Paul Judson.

6. Carved Out
The original title of the picture was 'Revelation' 1994. Artist: © Sophie Hacker.

7. Penitence
Artist: © Sister Ann Wilson OSB.

8. Healing
Artist: © Sophie Hacker.

9. After Great Pain
Artist: © Paul Judson.

10. Resurrection
The original title of the picture is 'Chalice' 1995.
Artist: © Sophie Hacker.

11. Peace
Artist: © Sister Rachel Clare.

12. The Fire of Love
Artist: © Paul Judson.

13. Water of Life
Artist: © Paul Judson.

14. The Shepherd
The original title of the picture is 'The Rainbow'.
Artist: © Margaret Neve, Montpelier Sandelson Gallery.

15. The Fish
Ref. Dom John Chapman, *Spiritual Letters* (Sheed & Ward, 1938): 'We are living in God in God's action, as a fish in water.' Artist: © Sister Anna SSM.

16. Reflection
Ref. Meister Eckhart, *Sermons and Treatises*, (London, DLT). Artist: © Sister Margaret Tournour RSCJ.

17. Rest
Ref. 'Listen to me, O house of Jacob, who have been borne by me from your birth; even to your old age I am he; even when you turn grey I will carry you' (Isaiah 46:3–4)
Artist: © Pauline K Green.

18. The Centre
Ref. Jesus said, 'Whenever you pray, go into your room and shut the door and pray to your Father who is in secret' (Matthew 6:6). Artist: © Mother Rosemary SLG.

19. Write on my Heart
Ref. 'On Detachment' in *Meister Eckhart, Deutsche Predigten und Traktate* (Munich, 1936). Quoted by Oliver Davies in *The Rhineland Mystics* (London, SPCK, 1989) p 39. Eckhart lived from 1260 to 1327.
Artist: © Sister Margaret Tournour RSCJ.

20. Nothing and Everything
Artist: © Graeme Bland.

21. The Seed
Ref. Words of Thomas Merton: 'To be a seed in the ground of one's life is to dissolve in the ground in order to become fruitful. One disappears into Love, in order to "be Love". To be fruitful in this sense one must forget every idea of fruitfulness or productivity, and merely be.' From the preface to the Japanese edition of *Thoughts in Solitude,* quoted by Esther de Waal in *A Seven-Day Journey with Thomas Merton* (Guildford, Eagle, 1992).
Artist: © Sister Margaret Tournour RSCJ.

22. Early Morning – A Fresh Beginning
Artist: © Sister Margaret Tournour RSCJ.

Calligraphy: All calligraphy © Kay Gibbons.

EXPLORING PRAYER SERIES

Guides to a richer prayer life for all
Series Editor: Joyce Huggett

Patterns Not Padlocks – *For parents and all busy people*
Angela Ashwin – 0 86347 0882

Patterns in Prayer (**tape**) **–** *Prayers and meditations with music*
Angela Ashwin – 0 86347 093 9

Finding God in the Fast Lane – *and in life's lay-by's*
Joyce Huggett – 0 86347 103X

Personality and Prayer – *Finding and extending the prayer style that suits your personality*
Ruth Fowke – 0 86347 209 5

Spiritual Friendship – *A guide for prayer companions and friends*
Wendy Miller – 0 86347 129 3

The Sounds of God – *Hearing the voice of God*
Michael Mitton – 0 86347 067 X

Finding The Still Point – *Making use of moods*
Gerald O'Mahony – 0 86347 110 2

Praying our Goodbyes – *The spirituality of change*
Joyce Rupp – 0 86347 154 4

Streams in Dry Land – *Praying when God is distant*
Heather Ward – 0 86347 104 8